PLANNING

STRATEGY OF

THE PROPHET [ﷺ]

Prof Javed Iqbal Saani
PhD, MBA (MIS), MBA (Finance), BBA

Intellectual Capital Enterprise
Limited, London

ISBN: 9781722129620

Published by Intellectual Capital Enterprise Limited
ICE Kemp House, 152-160 City Road
London, EC1 V2N
Printed in England

CONTENTS

VI

Say (to them, O Muhammad): Are those who know equal with those who know not? But only men of understanding will pay heed. [Az-Zumar: 9]

VIII

Anas (May Allah be pleased with him) reported:

The Messenger of Allah (ﷺ) said, "He who goes forth in search of knowledge is considered as struggling in the Cause of Allah until he returns."

[At- Tirmidhi].

x

Abu'd-Darda' (RA) said, "I heard the Messenger of Allah, may Allah bless him and grant him peace, say,

1. 'Allah will make the path to the Garden easy for anyone who travels a path in search of knowledge.

2. Angels spread their wings for the seeker of knowledge out of pleasure for what he is doing.

3. Everyone in the heavens and everyone in the earth asks forgiveness for a man of knowledge, even the fish in the water.

4. The superiority of the man of knowledge to the man of worship is like the superiority of the moon to all the planets.

5. The men of knowledge are the heirs of the Prophets.

6. The Prophets bequeath neither dinar nor dirham; they bequeath knowledge. Whoever takes it has taken an ample portion.'"

[Abu Dawud and at-Tirmidhi; Riyadh us Salihin, Hadith 1388, p. 211]

It was by the mercy of God that you were lenient with them (O Muhammad), for if you had been severe and hard-hearted, they would have forsaken you. So, pardon them and ask (God's) forgiveness for them and consult with them upon the conduct of affairs. [Al-e-Imran: 159]

Dedication

To the entire Ummah who have embraced the message of the prophet (ﷺ) and is sacrificing because they proclaim that Allah (SWT) is their Rubb, Quran is their book and Muhammad (ﷺ) is their prophet (ﷺ), the leader.

Acknowledgement

I am obliged to my family who spared me to embark on the project. They also provide valuable information which enriched the contents of this effort. May Allah reward them for their contribution? Ameen!

Preface

Allah (SWT), the exalted, the most gracious, the most merciful, the most knowledgeable, bestowed upon His message upon His most beloved creation, the leader of prophets (AS), benefactor of the humans and a blessing for both worlds. He is the source of guidance to seek the pleasure of our creator, the sustainer, and the controller of our affairs. He has shown the perfect path that leads towards paradise, the ultimate aboard of those who embrace the message of the truthful, sacrificed their lives and belongings for the purpose. The mercy of Allah (SWT) to the team of the prophet (ﷺ) who followed the noble footsteps of our and their beloved leader and offered everything that they had for the cause of Islam. It encompasses every sphere of human activity whether individual or collective at a small level or at a large level.

Mankind had been managing its affairs since the inception of life on the planet. Prophets were chosen people who received guidance from Allah (SWT) who is ever watching, knowing, and managing the universe. The knowledge of the prophets is extremely high which is not attainable by a common person. Each action they take, they did it with the guidance of Allah (SWT). So, there is no chance of mistake for them.

Since management science is one of the recent disciplines, therefore, little research has been conducted in Islamic perspective. This book is an attempt towards it. Contemporary managers manage their organisations on the bases of available knowledge and practices. Experts had divided their job into four well-known parts. Planning, organising, leading, and controlling. I have authored a research paper about planning in Islamic perspective in 2009 with one of my colleagues. It was a brief account of the subject. Therefore, I thought it needs expansion. Consequently, this small booklet emerged. In addition, one of my reviewers of one of my books on a similar subject suggested that small books must be produced based upon the life of the prophet(ﷺ). And it is the first effort towards it.

First four chapter is dealing with the subject with reference to various aspects of the life of the prophet (ﷺ). The fifth chapter is reserved to a specific instance; the case study. Managerial implications are the learning from the case study. Managers can apply them in the future planning endeavours.

Finally, if something is good for the reader it is the mercy and favour of Allah (SWT); however, all mistakes go to my account. I ask forgiveness from Allah (SWT) for this. He is merciful, I hope He would forgive me whether they are intentional or unintentional mistakes.

Professor Javed Iqbal Saani, Ph. D
Manchester
June 28, 2018

1 The premises of planning

Going concerns appoint managers to plan organizational matters. A given authority i.e. board of directors or board of trustees approves their job specifications and job descriptions. Managers assume their job according to these elements. Job specification describes the qualification and experience required for a job. The job description describes the details of duties and responsibilities related to the job.

Allah (SWT) has appointed his prophet (ﷺ) and He described the job descriptions. However, He has not implicitly described the job specifications because Allah (SWT) has instilled all the requirements or job specifications in the prophets (AS) and an apostle (AS). Allah had taught them these qualities as we can see from the life of the prophet (AS). Prophets (AS) used to learn these qualities from Allah and teach and convey to their nations. Islamic scholars believe that prophets (AS) required two weapons or tools for the job of prophethood: knowledge and strategy/wisdom. Allah (SWT) bestowed them upon the prophets (AS). Allah (SWT) also described the job descriptions for each of the prophet (AS). He trained them whenever it was necessary. All the prophets (AS) functioned as per their job descriptions.

We understand that manager's duties and responsibilities include planning, organizing, leading, and controlling. The division of duties and responsibilities into these four categories is for the facilitation and understanding of the managerial job.

We are examining a case of managerial activities that prophet Muhammad (ﷺ) had taken to manage his responsibility of introduction of Islam in the world. It also includes management of his organization (The first Islamic State of Madinah). It may be worthwhile to note that the job of the prophet (ﷺ) was the establishment of Islam. He did it in Makkah for about 13 years without a state.

Creation of a state was not his need. Islam spread from Makkah without the existence of a state. But Allah granted him the state as a reward to do the work of dawah. Most of the other prophets (AS) established their religions without a state. It implies that for the establishment of religion, or its revival does not require a state. We can observe this fact today. There are scores of Islamic states in the world today, but Islam does not exist in its true form in any of these states.

Meaning of planning[1]

Planning implies deciding in advance about the activities of an organisation. In business

---

[1] Robins and Coulter (2012) split the planning into three parts: decision making, planning and strategic management. They believe planning mean "defining the organization's goals, establishing strategies for achieving those goals, and developing plans to integrate and coordinate work activities. It is concerned with both ends (what) and means (how).
According to DeCenzo (2011) planning consists of two elements: goals and plan. For him "Goals (objectives) are desired outcomes or targets." He says, "They guide management decisions and form the criterion against which work results are measured. That is why they are often described as the essential elements of planning. Managers must know the desired target or outcome before you can establish plans for reaching it."

enterprises, managers make decisions about inputs, processing, and output. And about supply chain, customer, partner companies and governments. They take these decisions according to the grand policy, vision, mission, and objectives. In other words, managers think what the organisation wants and how it will achieve it.

There are some views of experts about the meaning of plan and planning. Let us examine them to gain an understanding of the matter. Plans are documents that outline how the organisation will achieve goals. They usually include <u>resource allocations, schedules, and other necessary actions to accomplish the goals</u>.

Planning is preparing a sequence of action steps to achieve some specific goal (Time Management Guide, 2015). In the words of Pea (2015) planning is a complex form of symbolic action that consists of consciously preconceiving a <u>sequence of actions</u> that will be sufficient for <u>achieving a goal</u>. Planning refers to deciding in advance about the project, product, human resources, and other activities. A manager must address at least five questions about the key areas.

What to do?

When to do?

Where to do?

How to do?

Who will do?

Modern management sciences offer tools, techniques, and strategies to determine each of these effectively and efficiently. The weapons did not develop at the time of the prophet (ﷺ) but he and his team have applied them. For instance, Iqbal and Ahmad (2009) have examined a planning strategy with respect to Hijrah expedition. They have applied a well-known strategy or planning model suggested by modern experts. Surprisingly, the prophet (ﷺ) had utilized all the steps involved in his Hijrah from Makkah to Madinah. It suggests that we can apply the same model to other examples which we are going to put forward here. In connection with the Hijrah expedition, the goal of the noble team was to reach Madinah for which they had undergone a series of steps. The steps were accurate and effective that lead them to achieve their goals without interruption.

Vision

The prophet (ﷺ) had an unclouded vision about his mission. According to the current meaning of the concept, vision is "an aspirational description of what an organization would like to achieve or accomplish in the mid-term or long-term future. It is intended to serve as a clear guide for choosing current and future courses of action." Allah (SWT) appointed the prophet (ﷺ) to serve the humanity which he visualised and described on many occasions. Once he told to Khabab bin Aret (RA) that be steadfast one-day Allah (SWT) would appoint you the leader of the world. He also predicted the dominance of Islam when Abu Zer (RA) took shelter under the umbrella of Islam. The prophet (ﷺ) said to him to the nearest effect that goes back to your tribe and comes back when we would get upper hand. Albeit it was the first phase of Islamic era (the secret period, when dawah was underway in homes and to the near relatives) but the prophet (ﷺ) had an unclouded vision about the success of his idea.

Similarly, once his daughter was worried about him due to the mischiefs of the infidels, the prophet (ﷺ) condoled her and said "do not worry, your father's religion would enter every home one day" At another occasion the disbeliever who perceived that the prophet (ﷺ) was offering a new religion to gain some worldly objectives. So, they offered wealth, leadership and women in lieu of stopping the job of dawah (Even many people believe the same today regarding the people who do some work of dawah). The prophet (ﷺ) rejected their offer and said if they put the sun on my one hand and the moon, on the other hand, I shall not stop this work. It came true shortly when the first Islamic state emerged on the globe. And Makkah fell to the hands of Muslims only after 18 years of the commencement of the effort. The key point to understand is the vision of the prophet (ﷺ) who visualised it years before the actual occurrence of the event.

Mission

The dictionary defines mission as "an organization's core purpose and focuses that normally remains unchanged over time ... it serves as filters to separate what is important from what is not, clearly state what will be served and how, and communicate a sense of intended direction to the entire organization." [1]

The prophet (ﷺ) announced his mission on the first day of open invitation. He said, "O people say Allah

---

[1]   http://www.businessdictionary.com/definition/mission-statement.html

is one, He is the only deity of worship, and you will be successful." Further, he said, "O people, I have been sent to warn you about a serious reprimand". The prophet (ﷺ) used both carrot and stick to motivate masses to consider Islam. It suggests that his mission was to convey the message of Allah (SWT) to the entire mankind. The prophet (ﷺ) remained focused on the mission in rest of his life. The destination was the pleasure of Allah (SWT). When a person accepts Islam as a way of life, he assumes obedience of Allah (SWT) and His prophet (ﷺ) in all occupations. He must perform the essentials of Islam: establishment of prayers five times a day, paying annual due (Zakat), fasting in Ramazan, and performing Hajj once in his life. And dealing with people according to the lifestyle of the prophet (ﷺ). It includes social, economic, and collective activities. The prophet (ﷺ) had demonstrated these aspects in his life. Allah (SWT) declared him the best example.

History became witnesses that he had shown the way of success in this world and in the Hereafter. He protected humanity from eternal disaster. His followers earned the respect and dignity in a brief period and became examples for the rest of mankind.

Objectives

We are discussing the life of the prophet (ﷺ) in managerial perspective in the contemporary environment, hence, we need to understand the phenomenon in current circumstances. I mean the primary target of the book is a manager who understands the managerial language. Therefore, we arrange the material accordingly. And we will solicit the help of contemporary experts of the field to do so. For instance, according to Decenzo (2011) planning consists of two elements: goals and plan. For him "Goals (objectives) are desired outcomes or targets." He says, "They guide management decisions and form the criterion against which work results are measured. That is why they are often described as the essential elements of planning. Managers must know the desired target or outcome before you can establish plans for reaching it."

Allah (SWT) has defined the goals for the prophet (ﷺ). The first goal was to learn or learn how to read. Allah (SWT) has described other goals in the following ayahs of the Quran.

1- "Read: In the name of your Lord Who creates, creates man from a clot." [Al-`Alaq: 1-2].

2-O thou wrapped up in thy raiment! Keep vigil the night long, save a little [Al-Muzammil: 1-2]

3-So, remember the name of thy Lord and devote thyself with a complete devotion [Al-Muzammil: 8]

4-And bear with patience what they utter, and part from them with a fair leave - taking. [Al-Muzammil: 10]

5-And seek forgiveness of Allah. [Al-Muzammil: 20]

However, the most important responsibility/objective was:

"O you who covers himself [with a garment], Arise and warn. And your Lord glorify. And your clothing purifies. And uncleanliness avoid. [Al-Muddaththir:1-5].

Allah (SWT) defined personal objectives in the first instance 1-5 above (Nevertheless, it is not an exhaustive list). And then He assigned a grand objective in surah Al-Muddaththir. Personal objectives worked as tools to achieve the grand objective.

Allah (SWT) had also assigned an associated objective:

And give glad tidings (O Muhammad) to those who believe and do good works; that theirs are Gardens underneath which rivers flow; as often as they are regaled, with food of the fruit thereof, they say: This is what was given us aforetime; and it is given to them in resemblance. There for them are pure companions; there forever they abide. [Al-Baqarah:25]

Some of the other glad tidings include:

•   Accept Islam you would get success in this world and in the Hereafter.

•   Pray salat (Namaz) and receive forgiveness

•   Pay zakat and purify your money

•   Fast in Ramadan and get taqwa i.e. Nearness to Allah (SWT)

•   Do hajj and be rich (Ghani)

•   Forgive others and get honoured

It suggests the key objective was to invite people towards Islam as described here. Say: This is my way: I call on God with sure knowledge, I and whoever follows me – Glory be to God! And I am not of the polytheists. [Yusuf: 108]

Allah (SWT) assigned the same mission/objective to all prophets (AS). The next question is how successfully the prophet (ﷺ) has achieved the objective. Allah (SWT) planned the way to achieve it and the prophet (ﷺ) implemented it.

2 What did he plan?

It is important to determine or plan the target market or the customer of the product the organisation is selling. When we look at the target market of the prophet (ﷺ), several individuals emerged. In other words, the prophet (ﷺ) had sold his idea to close relative and friends.

The prophet (ﷺ) put forward the new idea to his household, his loyal wife in the first instance. It was like test marketing. He proceeded to the close friend and a respectful personality of the city and Quraysh, Abu Bakker (RA).

Since it was the era of tribal life, therefore, the prophet (ﷺ) planned to present the idea to his tribe. The prophet (ﷺ) gathered Quraysh and offered the idea to them. He announced that Allah

(SWT) had appointed him as a prophet (ﷺ); I testify that Allah (SWT) is one, there is no deity of worship except Him. I invite you to accept it as I believe it. You would be successful in this world and honoured in the Hereafter. His argument was to ask people to embrace him as a prophet (ﷺ) and accept the supremacy of Allah (SWT) as the only to whom one worship. He invited towards one Allah because most of the people were worshipping multi gods, they were a polytheist.

There were a couple of things to do to introduce the new idea gradually. These were part of his plan. They include the following elements.

1.   First was to sell the new idea (product) to people (in business language to the new customers).

2.   Second to educate them about the idea.[1]

3.   Third to keep them (The new buyer of the idea) motivated to continue to own the new product.

4.   Fourth to inspire them to sell the idea to others.

---

[1] We use idea as an alternative to product as I have defined product in business language earlier.

5.   Finally, people of the surrounding areas would listen about the new idea; they would come to embrace the idea. How to deal with them?

We take them in turn to grab the core of the prophet's (ﷺ) planning strategy.

Sell the new idea.

He started 'work from home' or he sold the idea to his household. Remember that selling to the household was one of the difficult phases in the history of mankind. Many households did not buy the noble idea previously but the character of the prophet (ﷺ) was so high that the household accepted his proposal immediately.   Abu Baker (RA), Ali (RA) and others followed the noble family. The number reached forty when Umer (RA) took the oath of Islam.

Apart from these individual plans, the prophet (ﷺ) had planned to export the message in nearby areas. He planned to travel to Taif. He did not receive a warm response on the spot, but his tour became the cause of people of the city to seek refuge under the shade of Islam. He identified another opportunity of selling of his idea to pilgrims of the time. People used to visit the holy land on annual basis. He planned to approach them; it took long to get success in the area. But it became highly fruitful. The people of Madinah bought his message in the year ten of YP.

The prophet (ﷺ) also planned to approach other countries. Tafial Doosi came from Yamen and started efforts to spread Islam there. He was constantly concentrating on people on Hajj. He devoted his energies in Mina where people stay many days. Consequently, people of Madinah accepted his message in the year eleventh of his period.[1] The prophet (ﷺ) also sent two groups of Muslims to Abyssinia for their safety but it also included the silent dawah. When one after another two teams appeared in the country and started to live there. People asked why they were there. The team explained to them their reasons for leaving their country. It took an official shape when infidels of Makkah followed them to claim them. Hazrat Jaffar (RA) proclaimed in front of the king and his courtiers. Those who did not know about the Muslim team and their presence in the country also came to know about them. In addition to the

---

[1] Razi, Muhammad Wali (1987) Hadhi-e-Alam, Dharul-Ilm: Karachi.

ground due to which they sought refuge in the country. Subsequently, the king became Muslim.

Education of the idea

Education was necessary to explain the way the new idea is to use /practice. Similarly, new revelations were comping from Allah (SWT); they were supposed to convey to those who had adopted the new idea. They were also the source of motivation for everyone and were authenticating the prophethood of the presenter. Some of them were descending according to the circumstances that emerged with the passage of time. For instance, surah Lahab was revealed as an answer to the actions of Abu Lahab and his wife.

Therefore, a separate place was chosen to work as an office. It was near the Holy Masjid, inside the neighbourhood. People used to enter the street and could enter the home secretly. It was known as 'Home of Arqum (RA)'. The place was also appropriate for those who were travelling from nearby areas in search of the new religion (idea). It is the human behaviour that people want to own the new things. So, it was the demand of the time to sell them the product and educate them or train them how to use it.

The prophet (ﷺ) and his companions used this academy (The home of Arqum (RA)) as a centre for learning. Allah (SWT) ordained salat during this period. Existing and newcomers learned salat here. Since it was the meeting place thus, the prophet (ﷺ) used to announce new revelation in the home. The work of invitation towards the new religion was secret. The prophet (ﷺ) and his companions used to visit prospective people in their homes, or they visit the academy where the prophet (ﷺ) was explaining them, Islam. Hazrat Umer (RA) became Muslim in the home of Arqum (RA). Abuzer Ghaffari became Muslim here as well.

Motivated by the masses.

It was necessary to keep the followers motivated. The pages of history revealed that insignificant people reverted to their old religion after entering in it. The follower of Musa (AS) stood steadfast against the oppressor. They said to the nearest effect that we would not leave the religion of Musa (AS) under any circumstances. The same happened with the followers of the prophet (ﷺ). When he saw the persecutions of Yasir (RA) and his family, the prophet (ﷺ) used to say, be patient, the paradise would be your aboard. The prophet (ﷺ)

always motivates people on the bases of the life Hereafter. Umer (RA) once got worried about the provision of the prophet (ﷺ), he replied the worldly life is for infidels. The Hereafter is for us. (Kaandhlawi, 1997)

Inspiring companions to sell the idea to others.

If we examine from the business point of view, business owner/manager always want to expand his level of business. In terms of sale, in terms of reach to more geographical area and in terms of approaching more customer. They make the plan for it. For example, an increase in sales and profitability, entering new markets and identifying inexperienced users etc.

The business of the prophet (ﷺ) was international. Allah (SWT) granted him the entire world till the Day of Judgement. It implies his market was the whole globe which necessitates that he must think in the same manner. And he did. Abu Bakker (RA) came under the shade of Islam. The prophet (ﷺ) allowed him to invite others towards the new religion. Tofail Doosi (RA) embraced Islam and returned to his country (Yamen) where he invited his family to Islam. They accepted the new religion happily.

Managing new entrants

Another issue was to manage those who come from other areas/countries. They required the teaching of fundamentals, food, and residence while staying in Makkah. People like Abu Zer (RA) and Tofail Doosi (RA) came from far flung areas. The prophet (☪) had a plan to manage them.

People used to visit Makkah for assorted reasons; they stay either in the Haram or became gust of someone. Looking after gusts and visitors was part of the Arab culture. When Abu Zer (RA) came to Makkah for Islam, he stayed three days with Ali (RA) as a gust. The companions also teach Islam to the visitors and newcomers.

Nevertheless, in Madinah the situation was different. Islamic scholars believe that after the conquer of Makkah about 300 tribes embraced Islam. The plan to send women folk to the houses of the companions and the male folk would stay in the masjid. Thus, teaching and hospitality was the responsibility of the companions because there was no central system to manage these affairs.

3 Examples of planning in Makkah

The prophet (ﷺ) has planned a range of endeavours: business, management of migration, management of wars, integration of Helpers and Migrants and management of peace treaties. Let us examine some of them. Another book of the author discusses a more detailed account of the subject.[1]

---

[1] Prof Dr Javed Iqbal Saani (2017) Prophet Muhammad (ﷺ) as a planning expert, available on amazon (Paperback edition)

Hijrah

Since the migration was the most illustrious incident in the history of Islam and in fact in the history of the world because the incident transformed the fate of people for ever, therefore, it seems appropriate to describe it.

The prophet (ﷺ) stared planning for it when he invited the delegates of Madinah towards Islam during the Hajj. Fortunately, some of them embraced his message. A larger group took shelter under the shade of Islam later. When they came to know that Muslims were in hardship in Makkah, they invited them to Madinah to avoid the difficulties they were facing. Muslims started to leave Makkah individually or in small groups to avoid an open battle with the infidels. The prophet (ﷺ) left when most of the companions reached Madinah.

The journey itself was an example of the well-planned venture. Abu Bakar (RA) prepared two she camels for the journey; the prophet (ﷺ) decided to travel in a team that included a guide and Abu Bakar (RA). They hired a guide and adopted a new path. The team stayed in the cave Sour for three days to divert the attention of the enemy who was searching for them actively. The expedition seemed a well-planned endeavour which ended successfully.

Iqbal and Ahmad (2009) have examined a planning strategy with respect to Hijrah expedition. They have applied a well-known strategy or planning model suggested by modern experts. Surprisingly, the prophet (ﷺ) had utilized all the steps involved in his Hijrah from Makkah to Madinah. It suggests that we can apply the same model to other examples which we are going to put forward here. In connection with the Hijrah expedition, the goal of the noble team was to reach Madinah for which they had undergone a series of steps. The steps were accurate and effective that lead them to achieve their goals without interruption.

Business ventures

He has managed his business prior to the announcement of his prophethood. His foreign business trips were successful and generated a handsome profit for the parties concerned. The business partnership converted onto a life partnership with the business colleague. Here we can assume that he has done something special which produced extraordinary results. It shows he was a successful business manager despite he had applied only prevalent business techniques but with honesty. Because the prophet's (ﷺ) honesty was famous; it might be one of the causes of success.

Planning the mission of dawah

The principal job of the prophet (ﷺ) was to spread the religion of Islam in the world among jins (genie) and humans till the Day of Judgement.

We can divide his planning endeavours into two phases: the Makken phase and the Madinah phase. An alternative division is possible i.e. short-term (Less than one year) and long-term (More than three years). Some use medium term-planning that covers more than one year but less than three years. Anyway, whatever period one uses for planning, it is relating to the achievement of the objective.

Planning the efforts of dawah in Makkah

We have used Makken and Madinah period because the range of objectives varied during these periods. The prophet (ﷺ) had expanded the message of Allah at the individual level in Makkah in most of the instances. But he invited the rulers of other countries as a head of the state in

Madinah. He fought wars with opponents as a collective group while in Makkah he and his followers persecuted individually. The opponents made some efforts to eliminate the entire Muslim community in Makkah. Their purpose was to harm the prophet (ﷺ) so that when he would not be there than his followers would disappear or leave the new religion. However, when Muslim entered in the fold of Islam, he became determined to die as Muslim.

There was another example of such feelings. When Bilal (RA) received persecution from disbelievers, there were no collective efforts on the part of the Muslim community to rescue him. Abu Bakar (RA) bought his freedom. However, it would have been possible that he would have done it from the instruction of the prophet (ﷺ). Similarly, Yasir (RA) and his family received great torture from the infidels, but no one took collective action from the Muslim side because it was the Will of Allah (SWT). But the sense of collectiveness was there. Muslims made two migrations to Abyssinia in groups. The prophet (ﷺ) made hijra with Abu Bakker (RA).

The strategy of dawah (in general) was individual, the prophet (ﷺ) used to invite people on the one-o-one basis. There were instances of collective dawah which took place in the early days. The strategy did not work well; therefore, the prophet (ﷺ) shifted his efforts towards individual dawah.

The programme consisted of four phases:

1.   From the beginning to the third year of the prophet (ﷺ) [YP]
2.   From the third year to the fifth YP
3.   From year 5 to year the 10th YP
4.   From year 10 to the 13th YP

Let us examine the planning elements of the prophet (ﷺ) had articulated in each of these phases.

Secret promotion of his idea

From a managerial perspective, a product includes physical artefacts, services, and ideas. The prophet (ﷺ) was promoting a new idea, Islam (It was new for the sake of argument, however, as the Qura'n says to the nearest effect, Islam was the original name of all the heavenly religions, but people change its name according to their own will i.e. Christianity etc.).

4 Examples of planning endeavours in Madinah

The magnitude of work enormously increased in the new land. The variety of dawah responsibilities also boosted. It revealed from the examination of the life of the prophet (ﷺ) that he had planned a range of activities and projects. For example,

1. Settlement and integration of two distinct communities of migrants and Helpers of Madinah

2. Managing non-muslim tribes
3. Expansion of dawah at the state level
4. Tackling the opposition of Quraysh and other opponents
5. Implementation of sharia as and when revealed.
6. Managing affairs of the newly emerged state
7. Managing armed encounters

It was in addition to the basic functions that were on the table in Makkah. The prophet (ﷺ) had managed them whenever it deemed necessary. His style of management was the contingency model. The contingency manager address matters when they emerge on the horizon. Nevertheless, peace and harmony were the prime targets behind these efforts. A detailed analysis of these seems beyond the scope of this treatise; a keen observer can take them as fundamentals to discuss in desired details.

Settlement and integration of migrants in Madinah

The migrants and the Helpers were two different communities and possessed diverse cultures. Most of the migrants belonged to the elites of Makkah and they were traders by profession. The Helpers were peasants and belonged to ordinary people of their city. However, the formers displaced from their homeland while the later were living on their tribal heritage. The prophet (ﷺ) planned to integrate them in a systematic way. The migrants supposed to stay in Madinah forever, therefore, they need moral and financial help of the locals. The prophet (ﷺ) has kept the social status of migrants in mind while declaring them 'brothers'. He created the brotherhood that was entirely based upon Islam. The leaders or progeny of leaders became brothers of the same status. It was necessary because it was the part of human psychology. The Helpers had shown long lasting instances of generosity. They offered half of their belongings. But the migrants were not greedy. They accepted the bare minimum for as long as they enabled themselves to stand on their feet.

Managing non-muslim tribes

Individuals were the focus of management in Makkah; the political leadership was in the hands of Quraysh but the scenario in Madinah was different. There were Jews, Arab tribes, and

Helpers, and their confederates. The prophet (ﷺ) planned to extend his influence upon these elements. The Quraysh was a significant danger (and the time showed it that they were a real danger). They could use the forces of Madinah and surrounding areas to harm Muslims. The author of Hadi-e-Alam says,

> When they prophet (ﷺ) arrived in Madinah he realised that there were people of Bani Israel who were living there since centuries became jealous of Muslims. They had been confederates of Makens in the past as well. The Quraysh would take revenge for their insult (that Muslims left them safely and they had found a place for permanent residence). And these people could help them. It could create a danger for Muslims. So before, all that happened, something was to do.

It compelled the prophet (ﷺ) to plan to manage the circumstances. Therefore, he signed peace treaties with Jews and others. These movements offered security to Muslims and the neighbouring people.

Expansion of dawah at the state level

Since the key objective of the prophet (ﷺ) was to convey the message of Allah (SWT) to humanity, therefore, he planned to approach heads of states or their representatives. He dispatched his special envoys to them. Mobarikpuri has cited names of eight heads of states to whom the prophet (ﷺ) had sent letters of invitation towards Islam. He appointed ambassadors to deliver them in person. The prophet (ﷺ) dispatched most of these envoys following the famous treaty of Hodhabia. The pact provided peace from Quraysh who were the most active opponents. Look at the strategy of the prophet (ﷺ) that expansion took place after internal stability. Remember that he concentrated on internal security in the first instances. First to integrate migrants and Helpers and then peace treaties with Jews and other tribes of the area. It was the third step toward the process of establishing a long-standing system of government. In response to his invitations, many respondents accepted his message, other inspired and some remained deprived of from the eternal blessings of Islam. Allah (SWT) is the one who guides those who He wishes. May He include us among the guided folk. Ameen.

Implementation of sharia as and when revealed.

The grand plan of the prophet (ﷺ) also encompasses the introduction of new rules. In principle, most of the sharia revealed in Madinah. Slat was the only command that Allah (SWT) ordained in Makkah. Allah (SWT) had revealed responsibilities of Muslims gradually. For instance, the prophet (ﷺ) implemented the prohibition of alcohol in phases. The purpose was to make it easy for the masses to embrace. Although the companions were ready to accept any command. When the command of hijab revealed and announced in the marketplace, the women sat dawn and asked for the cloaks to wear and move. The same happened with the wine. As soon as the order delivered, people vomited out of their stomachs what they had drunk. The traders destroyed their possessions and so on.

Managing affairs of the newly emerged state

Mubarikpuri believes that when the peace pact was signed with the Jews of Madinah, the foundations of a federal government were laid dawn. According to the stipulations of the pact, the last resort shall be the prophet (ﷺ). Muslims were a collective force. The peace treaty was with the entire community of Islam rather than individuals. It implies the pact was between two communities, two nations with distinct religion, geographical area, and culture. Jews also accepted the prophet (ﷺ) as the supreme authority in case of any dispute between the signatories.

The communication with heads of other countries was based upon the same assumption that Madinah was now the first Muslim state on the surface of the earth. The treaty of Hodabia and subsequent agreements with Jews etc revealed the outcomes of it.

The system of zakat also introduced; both the collection and distribution of financial resources. Military encounters were part of it.

Armed encounters

The prophet (ﷺ) has led 27 battles where he participated himself. The prophet (ﷺ) almost won all of them. He needed three factors for these wars: Human resources, weapons and working capital i.e. day to day necessities. In addition, the commanders also need a strategy to utilize these resources. As an example, at the occasion of Tabuk war (or Ghazwa Tabuk) the prophet (ﷺ) made an announcement of it in response to the threat from the Roman king. People used to own their own weapons which imply the question of human capital and weapons was not under consideration. However, working capital was the need of the time. The Islamic government collected the donation for it. Therefore, requirements were on the table to move forward.

There was no collective programme of training at that time. It was the part of a child grooming that he learns how to use sword, arrow, and other prevalent armours. In this way, every soldier was 'home trained'. However, the prophet (ﷺ) used to keep extra weapons. Experts believed that 12 swards were in his possessions at the time of his eternal departure. They were part of the department of defence.

The third type of projects the prophet (ﷺ) dealt with was the political negotiation and arriving at appropriate treaties. The prophet had established a team of sahabah called shurah to make consultation whenever required. The same team decided the fate of the prisoners of Ghazwa Badr. The prophet (ﷺ) also planned the contents and other matters of various peace treaties with this team.

5 Case study - The Hijrah Journey

The case study is one of the popular methods of teaching and learning in management education. It seems appropriate to add such a study in this book to understand the phenomenon.

Since the migration was the most illustrious incident in the history of Islam and in fact in the history of the world because the incident transformed the fate of people for ever, therefore, it seems appropriate to describe it in this context.

Background

When the prophet (ﷺ) received the first revelation, his wife took him to one of the monks of the time, Warqa bin Nofil. Mobarikpuri (1995) writes,

"She set out with the Prophet (Peace be upon him) to her cousin Waraqa bin Nawfal bin Asad bin 'Abd Al- 'Uzza, who had embraced Christianity in the pre-Islamic period, and used to write the Bible in Hebrew. He was a blind old man. Khadijah said: "My cousin! Listen to your nephew!" Waraqa said: "O my nephew! What did you see?" The Messenger of Allâh (Peace be upon him) told him what had happened to him. Waraqa replied: "This is 'Namus' i.e. (the angel who is entrusted with Divine Secrets) that Allâh sent to Moses. I wish I were younger. I wish I could live up to the time when your people would turn you out." Muhammad (Peace be upon him) asked: "Will they drive me out?" Waraqa answered in the affirmative and said: "Anyone who came with something similar to what you have brought was treated with hostility; and if I should be alive till that day, then I would support you strongly." It implies that Hijrah was destined. The prophet (ﷺ) had to leave his cherished home and hometown. Quraysh had created difficult circumstances for the prophet (ﷺ) and his followers to remain in

Makkah. The prophet (ﷺ) was in search of an alternative place to continue his mission. He stared planning for it when he invited the delegates of Madinah towards Islam during the Hajj period. Fortunately, some of them embraced his message. A larger group took shelter under the shade of Islam later. When they came to know that Muslims were in hardship in Makkah, they invited them to Madinah to avoid the difficulties they were facing. Muslims started to leave Makkah individually or in small groups to avoid an open battle with the infidels.

Quraysh came to know about the plan of the prophet (ﷺ) to leave Makkah and settled down in Madinah, a safe place for him and his companions. The conspired for the assignation of the prophet (ﷺ). "Hadhrat Urwa narrates that after the Hajj season, Rasulullaah (ﷺ) was in Makkah during the remaining days of Dhulijjah, Muharram, and Safar. The Mushrikeen then gathered to conspire against him, thinking that he would soon be leaving Makkah since they knew that Allaah had created a place of safety and protection for him in Madinah. They had also found out that the Ansaar had accepted Islaam and that the Muhaajireen were going to them. The Mushrikeen, therefore, planned to capture Rasulullaah (ﷺ) and then either assassinate him, imprison him., exile him or keep him tied up. Allaah informed Rasulullaah (ﷺ) about their plot and revealed the following verse:

(O Muhammad (ﷺ) Remember the time) When the Kuffaar schemed against you to imprison you, kill you or exile you (drive you out of Makkah). They plan and Allaah plans. Allaah is the best of planners." (Surah Anfaal: 30)

The day when Rasulullaah (ﷺ) went to the house of Hadhrat Abu Bakr (رضي الله عنه), Nabi (ﷺ) was informed that the Mushrikeen planned to assassinate him as he slept that night."[1] It suggests that it was the right time to commence the sacred journey.

Preparation

Planning means deciding in advance. It includes the timing of action and arrangement of required resources. Allah (SWT) had decided the timing and Abu Bakr (رضي الله عنها) arranged the resources. Hadhrat Aiysha (رضي الله عنها) says, "Rasulullaah (ﷺ) said, 'Allaah has permitted me to migrate and to leave Makkah. Hadhrat Abu Bakr (رضي الله عنه), asked May I accompany you? Rasulullaah replied,

---

[1] Kaandhlawi (2012), p.339.

"Certainly," replied Rasulullaah (ﷺ). Hadhrat Abu Bakr (رضي الله عنه) said, "I have two camels that I have been rearing from a long time in anticipation for this day. You may take one." Rasulullaah (ﷺ) said, "Only at a price, Abu Bakr." Hadhrat Abu Bakr (رضي الله عنه) replied, "May my parents be sacrificed for you". You may have it at a price if you, so wish."[1] Thus, the required resources were available. The plan of the infidels to eliminate the source of guidance was about to fail. Allah (SWT) had a plan to eliminate kuffer from the sacred land forever. And it had happened.

The journey

The prophet (ﷺ) left when most of the companions reached Madinah. The journey itself was an example of a well-planned venture. Molana Yusaf Kandhelvi writes,

"Under the veil of the night, Rasulullaah (ﷺ) and Hadhrat Abu Bakr (رضي الله عنه) left for the cave in the Thowr mountain, which is mentioned in the holy Qur'aan. Hadhrat Ali bin Abi Taalib (رضي الله عنه) slept on Rasulullaah's (ﷺ) bed so that Rasulullaah (ﷺ)

---

[1] Kaandhlawi (2012), p.341.

could hide from Mushrikeen spies (who would think that Rasulullaah (ﷺ) is asleep in the house). The Mushrikeen spend the night walking about and discussing how they would leap on to the person sleeping and tie him up. They continued in this manner until dawn broke and they saw Hadhrat Ali (رضي الله عنه) stand up from Rasulullaah's (ﷺ) bed. When they asked Hadhrat Ali (رضي الله عنه) where Rasulullaah (ﷺ) was, he said that he did not know."

The reaction

They then realised that Rasulullaah (ﷺ) had left Makkah. Molana continues the topic, "The Mushrikeen then took to their mounts and started searching for Rasulullaah. (ﷺ). They also sent messages to the people at the various oases, instructing them to capture Rasulullaah (ﷺ) and promising them large rewards. They reached the cave of Thowr; here Rasulullaah (ﷺ) and Hadhrat Abu Bakr (رضي الله عنه) hid and had even climbed on top of the cave (where the entrance was). Rasulullaah (ﷺ) heard their voices and Hadhrat Abu Bakr (رضي الله عنه) became worried and frightened. Rasulullaah (ﷺ) then said to him.

"... Do not grieve (do not fear for my safety). Verily Allaah is with us (and He will protect us from the Kuffaar) ... " {Surah Taubah: 40)

Rasulullaah (ﷺ) then made du'aa to Allaah and Allaah sent peace and tranquillity to them as referred to in the following verse:

. . . So Allaah (SWT) caused His tranquillity (serenity, mercy, and peace) to descend on him, assisted him with an army (of angels and other creation) that you had not seen. And (Allaah (SWT)) placed the word of the Kuffaar (the call to Shirk) at the very bottom while the word of Allaah (the Kalimah) is right at the top. Allaah is Mighty, The Wise. {Surah Taubah: 40).

The enemy was searching continuously, in the words of Molan Yusaf Kandhelvi, "When they arrived at the cave, Hadhrat Abu Bakr (رضي الله عنه) entered first and placed his finger in every hole, fearing that there may be an insect there (which would harm Rasulullaah (ﷺ). When the Quraysh found out that they were gone, they set out in search of them and fixed a reward of a hundred camels for anyone who captured Rasulullaah (ﷺ). They scoured the mountains of Makkah and eventually reached the mountain where Rasulullaah (ﷺ) and Hadhrat Abu

Bakr (رضي الله عنه) were hiding. Referring to a person who was facing the cave, Hadhrat Abu Bakr (رضي الله عنه) said, "O Rasulullaah (ﷺ) they will surely see us." "Never," replied Rasulullaah (ﷺ), "because the angels are hiding us with their wings." Still facing the cave, the man then sat down to pass urine. Rasulullaah (ﷺ) said, "Had he seen-us, he would never have done that."[1] The noble team stayed there for three days.

He writes further about the journey. "Hadhrat Abu Bakr (رضي الله عنه) had several milk-giving goats that would be brought to him and taken to his family in Makkah. He also had an honest and trustworthy slave by the name of Hadhrat Aamir bin Fuhayra (رضي الله عنه) who was a particularly good Muslim. Hadhrat Abu Bakr (رضي الله عنه) sent him to hire a guide (to take them to Madinah) and Hadhrat Aamir (رضي الله عنه) hired a man called Ibnul Ayqadh. He belonged to the Banu Abd bin Adi tribe who were allies of the Banu Sahm branch of the Banu Aas bin Waa'il tribe that belonged to the Quraysh. This guide from the Banu Adi tribe was a Mushrik then and it was his occupation to guide people on the journeys. During those nights (that they hid the cave), the two of them (Hadhrat Aamir (رضي الله عنه)

---

[1] Kaandhlawi (2012), p.339-344.

and the guide) hid in the camels of Rasulullaah (ﷺ) and Hadhrat Abu Bakr (رضي الله عنه) while Hadhrat Abdullaah (رضي الله عنه) the son of Hadhrat Abu Bakr (رضي الله عنه) would come to them every evening and relate to them the events taking place in Makkah. Every night, Hadhrat Aamir (رضي الله عنه) would bring them some goats, which they would milk and then slaughter one to eat. Early in the mornings, he would take the goats away to the grazing fields that the people used for their goats and no one realised what was happening."[1]

Towards Madinah

"This continued until talk of Rasulullaah (ﷺ) and Hadhrat Abu Bakr (رضي الله عنه) died down and they learnt that things were quiet. Their two companions then arrived with the camels, and they left. They had already been in the cave for two days and two nights. They took Hadhrat Aamir bin Fuhayra (رضي الله عنه) along with them, who drove the camels, served them, and assisted them. Hadhrat Abu Bakr (رضي الله عنه) would let him ride the camel behind him in turns. Besides Hadhrat Aamir (رضي الله عنه) and the guide from the Banu Adi, no one else accompanied Rasulullaah (ﷺ) and Hadhrat Abu Bakr (رضي الله عنه).

---

[1] Kaandhlawi (2012), p.340-341.

(After three nights) Rasulullaah (ﷺ) and Hadhrat Abu Bakr (رضي الله عنه) left the cave and took a route along the coast. Hadhrat Abu Bakr (رضي الله عنه) travelled in front of Rasulullaah (ﷺ) but whenever he felt any danger from the rear, he travelled at the back. The entire journey passed in this manner. Hadhrat Abu Bakr (رضي الله عنه) was a well-known man. Therefore, whenever someone met him, they asked who was with him. He would reply, "He is a guide who is showing me the way." By saying this, he meant that Rasulullaah (ﷺ) was guiding him in Deen, but the person thought that Rasulullaah (ﷺ) was someone showing him the road. When they reached the settlement of Qudayd which lay on their route, someone told the Banu Mudlaj tribe (who lived there), "I have seen two riders near the coast. I think that they are the men from the Quraysh whom you are searching for." Suraaqa bin Maalik said to the person, "Those are two men whom we have sent out to do some work for the people." (Suraaqa knew that that the riders were Rasulullaah (ﷺ) and Hadhrat Abu Bakr (رضي الله عنه) said this so that he could have them to himself and earn the reward). Suraaqa then called for his slave woman and whispered to her to get his horse. He then set out on the trail of Rasulullaah (ﷺ) and Hadhrat Abu Bakr (رضي الله عنه).

Hadhrat Abu Bakr (رضي الله عنه) related, "We left (the cave) early at night and travelled speedily the entire day and night the afternoon when the heat became intense. I then strained my eye to see whether I could see any shade to take shelter. When I spotted a large boulder, I hurried to it and found that it still offered some shade. I then levelled the ground for Rasulullaah (ﷺ) and spread out a coat for him. I then bade him lie down and he did. Thereafter, I went to see whether I could spot anyone who was searching for us." Hadhrat Abu Bakr (رضي الله عنه) related further, "When I saw a shepherd and asked him who he worked for, he took the name of a man from the Quraysh whom I knew. 'Do any of the goats have milk?' I asked. Yes,' he replied. 'Will you milk some for me?' I enquired. When he agreed, he held the animal still as I had asked. I then asked him to wipe off the sand from the udders (which he did with his hands), and I then asked him to dust his hands off. I had a container with me that had a cloth tied to the mouth. After he had milked a bit of milk for me, I threw water onto a cup so that its bottom got cold (and the milk as well). I then went to Rasulullaah (ﷺ) and found

45

him awake. I said, 'Drink, O Rasulullaah (ﷺ). He then drank so much that I became incredibly pleased. 'Is it not time to leave?' I spoke. We then left."

"Although people were searching for us, no one caught up with us besides Suraaqa bin Maalik bin Ju'shum, who did so on his horse. (Seeing him approach), I said, "O Rasulullaah (ﷺ) here comes someone in search of us. He has caught up with us.' Rasulullaah (ﷺ) said, 'Do not grieve because Allah (SWT) is with us.' When Suraaqa drew close and was only the distance of one or two spear lengths away from us, I cried and said, 'O Rasulullaah (ﷺ), he has caught up with us!' Rasulullaah (ﷺ) said, 'What makes you weep?' I replied, 'I swear by Allah (SWT) that it is not for my own safety that I weep but I am crying for your safety. Rasulullaah (ﷺ) then made du'aa saying, 'O Allah (SWT)! Deal with him on our behalf as You please.' Suraaqa's horse suddenly sank into the ground up to its belly although the ground was hard. Suraaqa sprang off the horse and said, 'O Muhammad! I know that you have done this. Please pray to Allah (SWT) to save me from this predicament and I swear by Allah (SWT) that I shall throw every other tracker I meet off your trail. Take an arrow from my quiver here and when you pass by a certain place where you will see my camels and goats (show this arrow to the shepherds) and take whatever you need.' Rasulullaah (ﷺ) said, 'I have no need for that.' Rasulullaah (ﷺ) then made du'aa to Allah (SWT) and Suraaqa was freed. He then returned to his people." "Rasulullaah (ﷺ) and I continued until we reached Madinah where the people came to welcome him. They climbed the roofs on either side of the road as servants and children ran on the road saying, 'Allah (SWT) u Akbar! Rasulullaah (ﷺ) had arrived! Muhammad (ﷺ) has come!' When the people started quarrelling about who would be his host, Rasulullaah (ﷺ) said, 'I shall stay the night with the Banu Najjaar tribe who are the maternal relatives of Abdul Muttalib so that I may honour them.' The following morning, Rasulullaah (ﷺ) stayed where he was commanded to stay (by Allah (SWT))."[1]

Managerial implications

Planning always takes place in response to a certain event, the action of competitors, government regulations (or changes in them), or as a routine

---

[1] Kaandhlawi (2012), p.345-346.

matter on a periodic basis or in a contingency situation.

The plan can be short-term (up to one year), medium-term (one to three years), long-term (three to 5 or more years). Some are contingency plan which is made on a contingency basis. Issues are planned on daily, weekly, monthly, or quarterly basis.

The Hijrah project was a short-term but contingency plan. Although the prophet (ﷺ) was expecting it since long and mentally prepared for it. His strategic plan did include it.

Triggers for Hijrah

When he approached people of Madinah in Mina, he told them that he was in search of a safe place where he could do the work of dawah peacefully.

"Hadhrat Rabee'ah bin Ibaad (رضي الله عنه) narrates that he was a youngster with his father at Mina when Rasulullaah (ﷺ) stopped at the camps of various Arab tribes saying to them, "O people of this tribe! I am indeed Allaah's Rasul (ﷺ) to you, instructing you to worship Allaah Alone without ascribing any partners to Him and to forsake these idols that you worship. I further direct you to believe in me, to accept me and to offer me asylum so that I may clearly express that which Allaah has sent me with."[1] Secondly, he sent two groups of his companions to Abyssinia to save them from the difficulties of Makkah and to identify an alternate place for future endeavours. Thirdly, he visited Taif to extend dawah to the people and if they accept Islam, it could be a future base camp for him. Fourthly, he signed a treaty with the people of Madinah for the purpose. Consequently, many of his companions left Makkah for Madinah. Finally, and most important was the command of Allah (SWT) to leave his homeland for the cause of Islam. The previous Heavenly books also predicted his migration from Makkah because his nation did not allow him to continue his job in Makkah. We have seen in the above paragraph that Warqa bin Nofal said his nation would force him to leave his hometown.

Planning process

A planning process can be identified from the expedition. It is described in the following paragraphs.

---

[1] Kaandhlawi (2012), p.116.

The first **trigger** was the revelation of Allah (SWT) to migrate. It was in addition to the other triggers as described above. The command was the immediate cause which permitted the prophet (ﷺ) to initiate the action. The second step was the **visit** of the prophet (ﷺ) to Abu Bakr (رضي الله عنه) so that further steps might be taken. He went at a time when he usually did not do it. He used to visit during other hours of the day/night, but they were under normal conditions. However, the visit was urgent because the infidels made a large profit plan. The prophet (ﷺ) ensured that he should be alone to discuss the matter with Abu Bakr (رضي الله عنه). He asked him to clear the room so that he could talk about the issue. So, secrecy was important. Abu Bakr (رضي الله عنه) sought permission to accompany the prophet (ﷺ) which was granted. The meeting was the beginning to articulate the plan.

It was the first meeting of the prophet (ﷺ) with Abu Bakr (رضي الله عنه) in this connection. He informed him that Allah (SWT) granted permission to move ahead. It implies that the plan was drawn as a team effort. Other members included in the team were:

1. Ali ibn-e-Talib (رضي الله عنه) (Representative of Rasulullaah (ﷺ) in Makkah)

2. Abdullah bin Abu Bakr (رضي الله عنه) (Information officer)
3. Aamir bin Fuhayra (رضي الله عنه) (The Shepherd)
4. Ibnul Ayqadh (The guide)
5. Asma bint Abu Bakr (رضي الله عنها) (Food maker)

Necessary **resources** were arranged i.e. two she-camels were needed for the journey. Although Abu Bakr (رضي الله عنه) offered one to the prophet (ﷺ) he preferred to buy one.

The next issue was the right **timing** of departure from the home. The night was a better option; the infidels besieged the residence of the prophet (ﷺ). Therefore, he was waiting for the dark to leave his home. Eventually, he left his cherished home and went out in the middle of disbelievers. He picked up some sand and threw upon the enemy. Went to Abu Bakr (رضي الله عنه), both travelled towards the cave Thowr.

Decision making

The expedition suggests that the prophet (ﷺ) had made many important decisions. Decision making is a choice from available alternatives. A manager can develop three responses when he supposed to decide: do nothing, follow a routine response and design a nonprogrammed response. [1]

He decided to initiate the migration process soon after receiving the Devine command. He made quick decisions about the following matters or planned the project:

1. Conducted a meeting and formed the team
2. Arranged resources (Human and others)
3. Decided the timing of implementing the plan
4. Selected the path towards Madinah
5. Appointed Ali as his representative/successor in his home

All the decision he made were nonprogrammed type responses because all were unique in nature. And they were one-off decisions.

Motivation and organising.

Motivation is a psychological process that keeps people willing to continue support for an organisation or individual. It is a persuasive power. Managers motivate employees through monetary and non-monetary sources. According to Dyck and Neubert "managers attempt to get individuals to

---

[1] Dyck and Neubert, p. 203, 205.

pursue organisational objectives willingly and persistently."[1]

All the companions were self-motivated to obey whatever was ordained to them. Their purpose was to please Allah (SWT) who rewards a Muslim in this world and promises eternal success in the Hereafter in response to their obedience to His prophet (ﷺ) and His commands. Thus, it was a continuous source of motivation for the team members of Hijrah expedition. However, some motivational actions were necessary at a given time. For example, when Abu Bakr (رضي الله عنه) worried about the safety of the prophet (ﷺ) in the cave Thowr, the prophet (ﷺ) said as reported by "Hadhrat Hasan Basri ... that when Rasulullaah (ﷺ) and Hadhrat Abu Bakr (رضي الله عنه) went to the cave, the Quraysh came to search for Rasulullaah (ﷺ). However, when they saw that a spider had spun a web on the entrance, they concluded that no one could have entered the cave. Rasulullaah (ﷺ) was busy performing salaah and Hadhrat Abu Bakr (رضي الله عنه) was keeping watch when Hadhrat Abu Bakr (رضي الله عنه) said, "Here come your people in search for you. By Allaah! I have no concern for myself, but

---

[1] Dyck and Neubert p. 369.

I fear that I should not see anything unpleasant happen to you." Rasulullaah (ﷺ) comforted him saying, "O Abu Bakr! Do not fear for Allaah is with us."

Theo Haimann says, "Organising is the process of defining and grouping the activities of the enterprise and establishing the authority relationships among them."[1] Given that the prophet (ﷺ) had organised the human resources in a team. There were seven persons involved in the venture as indicated above. Three of them carried out the journey to Madinah: The prophet (ﷺ), Abu Bakr (رضي الله عنه) and the guide. He was controlling the entire endeavour which suggests that span of control[2] was 1 to 3 and 1 to 7.

Application of a planning model

Iqbal and Ahmad (2009) have examined a planning strategy with respect to Hijrah expedition. They have applied a well-known strategy or planning model

---

[1] Haimann, Theo and Raymond L. Hilgert (1972) Supervision: Concepts and Practices of Management, South-Western Publishing Company.

[2] "Span of control refers to the number of people that a manager can supervise." (Allen, Louis A. (1958) Management and organization, New York: McGraw-Hill.)

suggested by modern experts. Surprisingly, the prophet (ﷺ) had utilized all the steps involved in his Hijrah from Makkah to Madinah. In connection with the Hijrah expedition, the goal of the noble team was to reach Madinah for which they had undergone a series of steps. The steps were accurate and effective that lead them to achieve their goals without interruption. The model includes the following elements of planning. The related examples from Hijrah case study are described in the sub-bullet points.

1-Awareness of opportunities

   a) Searched the novel places for the future base camp of Islam such as Taif and Abyssinia.

   b) The Muslims of Madinah invited the prophet(ﷺ).

   c) Allah (SWT) commanded for migration.

2-Setting the objectives

   a) To obey Allah (SWT).
   b) To leave Makkah peacefully.
   c) To reach Madinah safely.
   d) To establish an Islamic state.
   e) To propagate Islam.

3-Planning premises (Assumptions)

a) The environment in Makkah was hostile and security of the prophet (ﷺ) and his companions were at risk.
b) The competition was tough, the enemy was trying to fail the plan i.e. progression of Islam.
c) Avoid encounter with the enemy because Allah (SWT) had not commanded for it yet.

4-Dtermining the alternatives

a) The first alternative was to leave Makkah and travel towards Madinah on the known path straightaway.
b) The second alternative was to stay in the suburb of Makkah for few days until a search died out and then start the journey towards Madinah on a less famous path.

5-Comparing alternatives

a) The second alternative was more promising in terms of assumptions and objectives.

6-Choosing the most promising alternative

b) The prophet (ﷺ) had chosen the second alternative.

7-Formulating supporting plans

The prophet (ﷺ) had drawn three supporting plans and implemented them:

a) Gathering and delivering information about the activities of the enemy.
b) Supply of food.
c) Removing footprints of travellers, information officer, and the food supplier.

8-Quantifying the plan

a) The prophet (ﷺ) bought a she-camel on credit for few hundred dinars (the legal tender of the time)
b) Other services were voluntary except some payment was made to the desert/Bedouin guide.

The case study suggests that the prophet (ﷺ) had planned the hijrah journey well because it had achieved its objectives. The success of a plan was to gain what was supposed to achieve. Five objectives were identified for the project. Three of them were achieved at the completion of the journey while remaining two were harvested with the passage of time. The pages of history tell us that they were also met.

\

6 Conclusion

Planning is one of the managerial functions of managers since long. The fundamental idea behind it was optimisation of organisational resources. It is possible when they are generated, utilised, and kept in reserve for future use. The purpose is to achieve the objectives of an organisation. Managers define objectives within the vision and mission of the organisation. The vision guides managers to conceptualise goals so that a strategy can be articulated to achieve them. Thus, a course of action is visualised at the start of an endeavour. It is like a railway track which does not allow the machine to derail from it. However, it is always a flexible strategy which can accommodate uncertain changes in the circumstances, availability of resources and stability of political and other factors.

An organisation is a part of the network of customer, suppliers, governmental bodies and public these days. It must operate within the competition which generates threats and sometimes provides opportunities for further development and advancement.

Let us look at the planning strategy of the prophet (ﷺ). His vision was noticeably clear from the start of his efforts. The prophet (ﷺ) instructed Abu Dharr (RA) as after inviting him towards Islam,

> Hadhrat Abu Dharr (رضي الله عنه) listened to Rasulullaah (ﷺ) and accepted Islaam on the spot. Rasulullaah (ﷺ) said to him, "Return to your people and convey the message to them until I send further instructions." ... **One day, Rasulullaah (ﷺ) said to me, 'Go back to your people and come to me when you hear that I am victorious.''**[1]

His mission was to convey the message of Allah (SWT) to mankind. He reiterated it on many

---

[1] Kaandhlawi (2012), p. 304, 307.

occasions. Almighty Allah (SWT) describes his mission, "Indeed you, [O Muhammad], are from among the messengers"[1] Massagers are sent down to convey the message of Allah, the exalted. <u>"O you who covers himself [with a garment], *Arise and warn*</u>"[2]

The prophet (ﷺ) had brought a revolution in the history of mankind. It does not happen without a structured plan. I have divided his planning endeavours into two periods. Because the demands of both were different. Propagation of his idea (the product in the business terms) in Makkah was limited under sever constraints. Protection of personnel who were functioning as "salespersons" was also one of the major concerns. He planned to protect them or at least some of them and sent them to the neighbouring country. Those who had adopted his message but left in Makkah were living under the state of fear and oppression. The prophet (ﷺ) motivated them to be patient and gave them glad tidings of eternal success.

---

[1] Surah Yasin: 3.
[2] Al-Muddaththir: 1 and 2.

However, the member of his teams was increasing gradually. It offered him and his existing colleagues a sense of encouragement. A successful leader keeps his followers motivated and prepared them for sacrifice for his cause. The prophet (ﷺ) did it. Not a single follower left him in limbo. Difficulties were on the way to every Muslim even the prominent figures such as Usman (رضي الله عنه) was suffering. "Hadhrat Muhammad bin Ibraheem Taymi narrates that when Hadhrat Uthmaan bin Affaan (رضي الله عنه) accepted Islaam, his uncle Hakam bin Abil Aas bin Umayyah securely bound him in ropes. He then said to Hadhrat Uthmaan (رضي الله عنه), "Have you turned away from the creed of your forefathers and turned to a new religion?" I swear by Allah (SWT) that I shall never release you until you forsake the religion you follow." Hadhrat Uthmaan (رضي الله عنه) replied, "I swear by Allah (SWT) that I shall never leave it." When Hakam saw how steadfast Hadhrat Uthmaan (رضي الله عنه) was in his religion, he released him."[1] Usman (رضي الله عنه) had to migrate to Abyssinia with his wife who was the daughter of the prophet (ﷺ).

The strategy of planning was a little bit different in in Madinah. Here plans were made to integrate

---

[1] Kaandhlawi (2012), p. 297.

Migrants and Helpers in the first instance to form a new community. Treaties were made with Jews and others to establish peace in Madinah and surrounding areas. It helped Muslims to focus on external enemies. Plans were articulated to run the affairs of the new state that emerged. Quraysh was a constant threat who imposed three battles upon Muslims. They were conspiring continuously to harm Muslims, so external issues of security were there. The primary part of the planning strategy was to avoid any military encounter but when the enemy invaded the Muslims, they had to defend themselves. Badr and Khandiq were live examples. In addition, the commands of Sharia were revealed; the prophet (ﷺ) had to implement them. Some were revealed gradually as the command of wine was sent down. Others were transmitted abruptly, all of them needed a strategy to implement. The prophet (ﷺ) had designed and implanted it amicably.

It was the time of expansion of Islamic idea. The prophet (ﷺ) approached Persian and Roman kings through correspondence. They were invited towards eternal peace and tranquillity of Islam.

Performance of planning is usually measured in terms of the objective it achieved within the framework of vision and mission. The pages of history witnessed that the prophet (ﷺ) had achieved all the objectives of his planning endeavours peacefully. He had transmitted the message of his creator with remarkable success. The impacts of it are felt today after centuries and would continue till the end of the Time.

Bibliography

Adair, John (2010) The Leadership of Muhammad (pbuh), New Delhi: Kogan Page India Private Limited.

Al-Bahaqi, Abi Bakker Ahmad Al-Hussain (2009) Dhalail Al-Nabuwwa, Karachi: Dharul Ishaat.

Allen, Louis A. (1958) Management and organization, New York: McGraw-Hill.

DeCenzo, David A. and Stephen P. Robbins (2010) Human Resource Management, New York: John Wiley & Sons.

Dess, Gregory G., G. T. Lumpkin, Alan B. Eisner (2006) Strategic Management: Text and Cases, New York: Irwin/McGraw-Hill.

Dyck, B and Mitchell J Neubert (2009) Principal of Management, South-Western.

Haimann, Theo and Raymond L. Hilgert (1972) Supervision: Concepts and Practices of Management, South-Western Publishing Company.

Hameed Ullah, M. (2006) The Prophet's (ﷺ) Establishing a State and his Succession, Beacon Books: Lahore.

Iqbal, Javed, and Muhammad Mushtaq Ahmad (2009) Planning in the Islamic Tradition: The Case of Hijrah Expedition, INSIGHTS 01(3), 37-68.

Kaandhlawi, Muhammad Zakarya (1997), Fazail-e-Amaal, Lahore: Kutibkhana Faizi.

Kaandhlawi, Muhammad Yusaf (2012), Hayatus Sahabah, Delhi: Islamic Books Services.

Koontz, Harold, and Heinz Weihrich (2006) Essentials of Management, New Delhi: Tata McGraw-Hill Education, pp. 81-84.

Kreitner, R (2009) Principal of Management, South-Western.

Lings, M M (1994) Muhammad, his life based on the earliest sources, Lahore: Suhail Academy.

Mubarakpuri, Safiur Rahman (1995) "The Sealed Nectar" (Ar-Raheeq Al-Makhtum), Lahore: Al-Maktba Alsalfia.

Nadvi, Sulaiman Hussaini (2205) Khutbat-e-Seerat, Karachi: Zam-Zam Publishers.

Noamani, Shibli and Syed Solaiman Nadhvi (2004) Seeratun-Nabi, Karachi: Dharul-Ishaat.

Pea, Roy D. (2015) What Is Planning Development the Development of? Accessed: April 2015, http://web.stanford.edu/~roypea/RoyPDF%20fold er/A11_Pea_82d.pdf

Phalwari, Muhammad Jaafer (1995) Peghambr-e-Insaniat, Lahore: Idara Sakafat-e-Islamia.

Razi, Muhammad Wali (1987) Hadhi-e-Alam, Dharul-Ilm: Karachi.

Robbins, Stephen, and Mary Coulter (2017) Management, New Delhi: Pearson Education.

Saani, Javed Iqbal (2017) Prophet Muhammad (ﷺ) as a planning expert, London: Intellectual Capital Enterprise Limited.

Siddiqi, Naeem (1997) The Benefactor of Humanity (Mohsin-e-Insaniyat), Dehli: Markazi Matabah Islami Publishers.

Tiem Management Guide (2015) What is planning and why you need to plan, Accessed: April 2015, http://www.time-management-guide.com/planning.html

INDEX

ABOUT THE AUTHOR

Dr. Javed Iqbal belongs to Rawalakot district Poonch Azad Kashmir. He received his early education from Pilot High School Rawalakot and received his matriculation in 1975 and intermediate from Hussain Shaheed Degree College of the same town. He earned BBA with a gold medal and an MBA with a gold medal from Azad Jammu and Kashmir University in 1986. He was appointed as a lecturer in Business Administration in the same university. Later, he was selected by the government of Pakistan for higher studies and deputed to the United Kingdom. He received MBA from the University of Hull and PhD from the University of Salford. Dr Iqbal has been working in England in various capacities: professor, director of studies, marketing advisor and academic advisor. Dr Iqbal returned to Home in 2006 and joined Iqra University Islamabad campus as an associate professor. He became the head of department of technology Management in International Islamic University Islamabad (IIUI). He went back to England for some time and re-joined IIUI in 2012. He is a Professor of Business Administration in Iqra

University, Islamabad and an Adjunct Professor in the School of Management in Asia e University Malaysia these days.

He is a distinguished teacher and world known scholar. His article title "Learning from a Doctoral Research Project: Structure and Content of a Research Proposal" has been ranked by one of the professors at Deakin University Australia as the best piece of knowledge for doctoral students on the subject. This paper is widely used and referred all over the world. Dr. Javed Iqbal has been nominated by an international organization for the Award of Distinguished Scientist for his research contribution. His books on various subjects are available on amazon.

OTHER BOOKS BY THE AUTHOR (S)

1. Prof Dr. Javed Iqbal Saani (2018) Qualities of Momins: The Quranic Perspective, Intellectual Capital Enterprise Limited, London, available on amazon (Paperback edition)

2. Prof Dr. Javed Iqbal Saani (2018) Hajj Experience: Combining Dawah and Manasiks, Intellectual Capital Enterprise Limited, London, available on amazon (Paperback edition)

3. Prof Dr. Javed Iqbal Saani (2018) Sukhn-e-Saani (The book of poetry), Intellectual Capital Enterprise Limited, London, available on amazon (Paperback edition)

4. Prof Dr. Javed Iqbal Saani (2018) Managing Your Projects, Intellectual Capital Enterprise Limited, London, available on amazon.co.uk. (Paperback edition)

5. Prof Dr. Javed Iqbal Saani (2017) Business Case Studies, Intellectual Capital Enterprise Limited, London, available on amazon (Paperback edition)

6. Prof Dr. Javed Iqbal Saani (2017) Virtues of Sickness: Selected Ahadith, available on amazon (Paperback edition)

7. Prof Dr. Javed Iqbal Saani (2017) Prophet Muhammad (ﷺ) as a planning expert, available on amazon (Paperback edition)

8. Prof Dr Javed Iqbal Saani (2017) Muhammad (ﷺ): His Trials & Tribulations, available on amazon (Paperback edition)

9. Prof Dr. Javed Iqbal Saani (2017) Sales and Marketing: Selected Ahadith, available on amazon.co.uk. (Paperback edition)

10. Prof Dr. Javed Iqbal Saani (2016) Research Proposals: Contents & Exemplars, available on amazon.co.uk. (Paperback edition)

11. Prof Dr. Javed Iqbal Saani (2016) Responsibilities of Managers: Selected Ahadith, available on amazon.co.uk. (Paperback edition)

12. Prof Dr. Javed Iqbal Saani (2016) Experience: The Journey of My Life, available on amazon.co.uk. (Paperback edition)

13. Prof Dr. Javed Iqbal Saani (2012) Understanding Information Systems, Manchester: GRaASS.

14. Prof Dr Javed Iqbal Saani (2011) Digital Divide in South Asia ISBN: 9789699578120.

15. Prof Dr. Javed Iqbal Saani and Muhammad Rafi Khattak (2011) Managing Risk in Projects, ISBN: 9789699578090.

16. Prof Dr. Javed Iqbal Saani and Muhammad Nadeem Khan (2011) Understanding Project Management, ISBN: 978969957845, available on amazon (Paperback edition)

17. Prof Dr. Javed Iqbal Saani (2011) Information Systems for Managers, Grass Books, Manchester.

18. Prof Dr. Javed Iqbal Saani (2010) Managing strategic change: a real-world case study, ISBN: 978-3838330952, available on amazon.co.uk. (Paperback edition)

[Please see the images of these books on the following pages in addition to my doctoral thesis]

PROPHET MUHAMMAD

AS A PLANNING EXPERT

PROF JAVED IQBAL SAANI, PHD

Sales & Marketing: Selected Ahadith

Javed Iqbal Saani

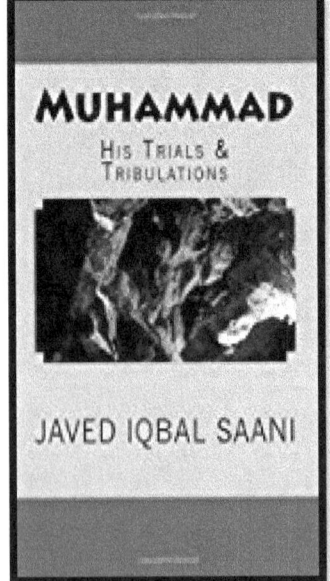

MUHAMMAD

HIS TRIALS & TRIBULATIONS

JAVED IQBAL SAANI

Responsibilities of Managers

Selected Ahadiths

Javed Iqbal Saani

Virtues of
Sickness
Selected Ahadith

Prof Javed Iqbal Saani, PhD

RESEARCH
PROPOSALS

CONTENTS &
EXEMPLARS

PROF JAVED
IQBAL SAANI, PHD

UNDERSTANDING
PROJECT
MANAGEMENT

PROF JAVED IQBAL SAANI
MUHAMMAD NADEEM KHAN

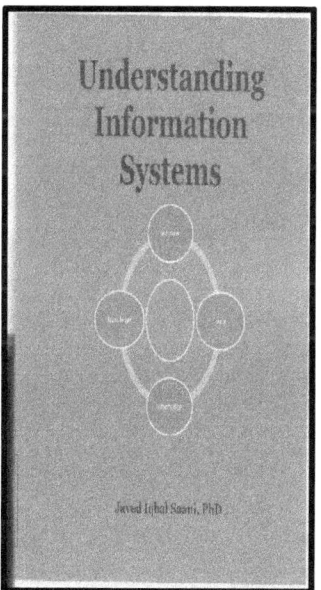

Understanding
Information
Systems

Javed Iqbal Saani, PhD

MANAGING
RISK IN
PROJECTS

Dr. Javed Iqbal Saani, PhD
Muhammad Rafi Khattak

Digital Divide
in
South Asia

Dr. Javed Iqbal, PhD

Business
Case Studies

Prof Javed Iqbal
Saani PhD

Hajj Experience
Combining Dawah
and Manasiks

Prof Dr Javed Iqbal Saani

NOTES

www.ingramcontent.com/pod-product-compliance
Lightning Source LLC
Chambersburg PA
CBHW071210220526
45468CB00002B/561